AF334443

ENDOMETRIOSIS COOKBOOK

MEGA BUNDLE – 4 Manuscripts in 1 – 160+ Endometriosis - friendly recipes including casseroles, stew, side dishes, and pasta recipes

TABLE OF CONTENTS

SIDE DISHES 10

FRIED VEGETABLES..10

ONION SAUCE 12

FISH "CAKE" 13

SUSHI HANDROLLS 14

STEAMED VEGETABLES 15

GUACAMOLE 16

CHICKEN NACHOS 17

SCRAMBLED EGGS WITH SALMON..............................18

CHICKEN WITH RICE 19

ROASTED VEGETABLES...20

SAUSAGE PIZZA 21

HEALTY PIZZA 22

SLAW 23

EDAMAME FRITATTA 24

ONION FRITATTA..25

LEAF FRITATTA 26

KALE FRITATTA 27

JICAMA FRITATTA...28

BROCCOLI FRITATTA..29

CAULIFLOWER SANDWICH 30

AVOCADO BOATS 31

MEXICAN CORN DIP 32

LEEK QUICHE 33

ROASTED SQUASH...34

BRUSSELS SPROUT CHIPS 35

CUCUMBER CHIPS 36

SQUASH CHIPS 37

PASTA 38

SIMPLE SPAGHETTI 38

SHRIMP PASTA 40

PASTA WITH OLIVES AND TOMATOES 41

SALAD 42

MORNING SALAD 42

TOMATO SOUP 43

CRAB SALAD 44

ASIAN SALAD 45

CHICKEN SALAD 46

CUCUMBER SALAD 47

GRAPEFRUIT SALAD 48

APPLE SALAD 49

COLESLAW 50

LOBSTER SALAD 51

RADISH SALAD 52

SPINACH SALAD 53

SECOND COOKBOOK 54

BREAKFAST 55

BEANS OMELETTE 55

ASIAN GREENS OMELETTE 56

BEANS OMELETTE 57

CABBAGE OMELETTE 58

MUSHROOM OMELETTE 59

TOMATO OMELETTE 60

OATS WITH PEANUT BUTTER 61

BREAKFAST GRANOLA 62

BANANA PANCAKES 63

LIME PANCAKES 64

GUAVA PANCAKES 65

APRICOT MUFFINS 66

PEACH MUFFINS..67

BLUEBERRY MUFFINS 68

PAPAYA MUFFINS..69

CORN OMELETTE 70

MUSHROOM OMELETTE 71

YAMS OMELETTE 72

RAISIN BREAKFAST MIX 73

SAUSAGE BREAKFAST SANDWICH 74

STRAWBERRY MUFFINS 75

LEEK FRITATTA..76

KALE FRITATTA 77

GREENS FRITATTA 78

BROCCOLI FRITATTA..79

DESSERTS 80

BREAKFAST COOKIES..80

BLUEBERRY PIE 81

PUMPKIN PIE..82

RICOTTA ICE-CREAM 83

SAFFRON ICE-CREAM 84

SMOOTHIES 85

TURMERIC-MANGO SMOOTHIE 85

AVOCADO-KALE SMOOTHIE 86

BUTTERMILK SMOOTHIE 87

GREEN SMOOTHIE...88

FRUIT SMOOTHIE 89

MANGO SMOOTHIE 90

DREAMSICLE SMOOTHIE 91

FIG SMOOTHIE 92

POMEGRANATE SMOOTHIE 93

GINGER-KALE SMOOTHIE 94

THIRD COOKBOOK...95

SOUP RECIPES 96

CAULIFLOWER SOUP 96

MUSHROOM SOUP 97

ZUCCHINI SOUP 98

CELERY SOUP...99

CARROT SOUP 100

CUCUMBER SOUP 101

SIDE DISHES 102

GOAT'S CHEESE RAREBIT 102

SMOKED MACKEREL PATE...104

PESTO CREAM VEGGIE DIP 105

CAULIFLOWER CHEESE 106

PUMPKIN RISOTTO 107

GREEN PESTO PASTA 108

MINCE WITH BASIL..109

PORK CHOPS 110

BEEF BURGERS 111

BAKED FISH 112

MINT COUSCOUS 113

FRESH PORK PATTIES...114

POTATO SALAD 115

LEBANESE BEAN SALAD 116

KALE & FENNEL SALAD 117

TOMATO & SPINACH SALAD 118

WILD RICE SALAD 119

KALE SALAD 120

THAI MANGO SALAD 121

HERBED SALAD 122

BEET SALAD 123

PEPITAS AND CRANBERRIES SALAD 124

FIESTA SHRIMP 125

CAULIFLOWER FRITTERS 126

FRENCH TOAST SANDWICHES 128

GREEK MIXED VEGETABLES 129

GRILLED SALMON STEAKS 131

ORIENTAL GREENS 132

BROCCOLI CASSEROLE 133

BEAN FRITATTA 134

ROASTED SQUASH 135

POTATO CHIPS 136

PIZZA 137

ZUCCHINI PIZZA 137

TUSCAN PIZZA 138

MARGHERITA PIZZA 139

SHAKSHUKA PIZZA 140

FOURTH COOKBOOK 141

ROAST RECIPES 142

ROASTED SQUASH 142

ROASTED CARROT 142

SOUP RECIPES 143

ZUCCHINI SOUP 143

SIDE DISHES 144

CHICKEN NUGGETS 144

BEEF FAJITAS 145

SUMMER SALMON 146

GRILLED SALMON 147

MONKFISH MUSSEL KEBABS 149

POTATO TORTILLA 151

ASIAN STIR-FRY 152

APRICOT CHICKEN PATTIES 153

GREEN PESTO PASTA 154

SALMON WITH ROSEMAY 155

MUSHROOM BURGERS 156

BLACK BEANS BURGERS 158

CABBAGE FRITATTA 160

BRUSSEL SPROUTS FRITATTA 161

CELERY FRITATTA 162

PROSCIUTTO FRITATTA 163

OREGANO FRITATTA 164

HUMMUS WRAP 165

POTATO WEDGES 166

KALE CHIPS 167

EGG ROLL BOWL 168

GREEK BOWL 169

CRANBERRY SALAD 170

GAZPACHO SALAD 171

RADISH & PARSLEY SALAD 172

ZUCCHINI & BELL PEPPER SALAD 173

QUINOA & AVOCADO SALAD 174

TOFU SALAD 175

PAD THAI SALAD...176

AVOCADO SALAD 177

MUSHROOM SALAD 178

MIXED GREENS SALAD 179

QUINOA SALAD 180

STEW RECIPES 181

FISH STEW 181

BUTTERNUT SQUASH STEW 183

CASSEROLE RECIPES 185

BACON CASSEROLE 185

ENCHILADA CASSEROLE 187

PIZZA RECIPES 189

CASSEROLE PIZZA 189

equally by a Committee of the American Bar Association and a Committee of Publishers and Associations.

In no way is it legal to reproduce, duplicate, or transmit any part of this document in either electronic means or in printed format. Recording of this publication is strictly prohibited and any storage of this document is not allowed unless with written permission from the publisher. All rights reserved.

The information provided herein is stated to be truthful and consistent, in that any liability, in terms of inattention or otherwise, by any usage or abuse of any policies, processes, or directions contained within is the solitary and utter responsibility of the recipient reader. Under no circumstances will any legal responsibility or blame be held against the publisher for any reparation, damages, or monetary loss due to the information herein, either directly or indirectly.

Respective authors own all copyrights not held by the publisher.

The information herein is offered for informational purposes solely, and is universal as so. The presentation of the information is without contract or any type of guarantee assurance.

The trademarks that are used are without any consent, and the publication of the trademark is without permission or backing by the trademark owner. All trademarks and brands within this book are for clarifying purposes only and are the owned by the owners themselves, not affiliated with this document.

Introduction

Endometriosis recipes for personal enjoyment but also for family enjoyment. You will love them for sure for how easy it is to prepare them.

FRIED VEGETABLES

Serves: **2**

Prep Time: **10**   Minutes

Cook Time: **15**   Minutes

Total Time: **25**   Minutes

INGREDIENTS

- 1 cup red bell pepper
- ¼ cup cucumber
- ¼ cup zucchini
- ¼ cup asparagus
- ¼ cup carrots
- 1 onion
- 2 eggs
- 1 tsp salt
- 1 tsp pepper
- Seasoning
- 1 tablespoon olive oil

DIRECTIONS

1. In a skillet heat olive oil and sauté onion until soft
2. Chop vegetables into thin slices and pour over onion
3. Whisk eggs with salt and pepper and pour over the vegetables
4. Cook until vegetables are brown
5. When ready remove from heat and serve

Serves: *4*
Prep Time: *10*   Minutes

Cook Time: *55*   Minutes

Total Time: *65*   Minutes

INGREDIENTS

- 1 onion
- 2 garlic cloves
- ¼ lb. carrots
- 1 potato
- 1 tablespoon balsamic vinegar
- ¼ tsp salt
- ¼ tsp black pepper
- 1 tablespoon olive oil
- 1 cup water

DIRECTIONS

1. Chop all the vegetables and place them in a heated skillet
2. Add remaining ingredients and cook on low heat
3. Allow to simmer for 40-45 minutes or until vegetables are soft
4. Transfer mixture to a blender and blend until smooth
5. When ready remove from the blender and serve

FISH "CAKE"

Serves: **4-6**

Prep Time: **10**   Minutes

Cook Time: **50**   Minutes

Total Time: **60**   Minutes

INGREDIENTS

- 2 tuna tins
- 2 potatoes
- 2 eggs
- 1 handful of gluten free flour
- 1 handful of parsley
- black pepper
- 1 cup breadcrumbs

DIRECTIONS

1. Preheat the oven to 350 F
2. Boil the potatoes until they are soft
3. Mix the tuna with parsley, black pepper and salt
4. Roll fish into patties and dip into a bowl with flour, then eggs and then breadcrumbs
5. Place the patties on a baking tray
6. Bake at 350 F for 40-45 minutes
7. When ready remove from heat and serve

Serves: 2
Prep Time: **10**   Minutes

Cook Time: **25**   Minutes

Total Time: **35**   Minutes

INGREDIENTS

- 1 sushi nori packet
- 4 tablespoons mayonnaise
- ½ lb. smoked salmon
- 1 tsp wasabi
- 1 cup cooked sushi rice
- 1 avocado

DIRECTIONS

1. Cut avocado and into thin slices
2. Take a sheet of sushi and spread mayonnaise onto the sheet
3. Add rice, salmon and avocado
4. Roll and dip sushi into wasabi and serve

Serves: *2*
Prep Time: *10*   Minutes

Cook Time: *10*   Minutes

Total Time: *20*   Minutes

INGREDIENTS

- 1 carrot
- 2 sweet potato
- 2 parsnips
- 1 zucchini
- 2 broccoli stems

DIRECTIONS

1. Chop vegetables into thin slices
2. Place all the vegetables into a steamer
3. Add enough water and cook on high until vegetables are steamed
4. When ready remove from the steamer and serve

Serves: 2

Prep Time: 5 Minutes

Cook Time: 5 Minutes

Total Time: *10* Minutes

INGREDIENTS

- 1 avocado
- 1 lime juice
- 1 handful of coriander
- 1 tsp olive oil
- 1 tsp salt
- 1 tsp pepper

DIRECTIONS

1. Place all the ingredients in a blender
2. Blend until smooth and transfer to a bowl

Serves: **4-6**

Prep Time: **15**   Minutes

Cook Time: **35**   Minutes

Total Time: **50**   Minutes

INGREDIENTS

- 2 chicken breasts
- Tortilla chips
- Fajita seasoning
- ¼ cup cheddar cheese
- 4-5 mushrooms
- Guacamole
- ¼ cup peppers

DIRECTIONS

1. In a pan heat olive oil and add chopped onion, sauté until soft
2. Add chicken, fajita seasoning and remaining vegetables
3. Cook on low heat for 10-12 minutes
4. Place tortilla chips into a baking dish, sprinkle cheese and bake in the oven until cheese has melted
5. Remove from the oven pour sautéed vegetables and chicken over and tortilla chips and serve

Serves: *2*

Prep Time: *10*   Minutes

Cook Time: *20*   Minutes

Total Time: *30*   Minutes

INGREDIENTS

- ½ lb. smoked salmon
- 2 eggs
- 1 avocado
- 1 tsp salt
- 1 tsp pepper
- 1 tps olive oil

DIRECTIONS

1. In a bowl whisk the eggs with salt and pepper
2. In a skillet heat olive oil and pour the egg mixture
3. Add salmon pieces to the mixture and cook for 2-3 minutes per side
4. When ready remove from the skillet, add avocado and serve

Serves: **4**

Prep Time: **10** Minutes

Cook Time: **25** Minutes

Total Time: **35** Minutes

INGREDIENTS

- 2 chicken breasts
- 1 cup cooked white rice
- 2 tablespoons mayonnaise
- 1 tablespoon curry powder
- 1 zucchini
- 1 cup broccoli
- 1 tablespoon olive oil

DIRECTIONS

1. Cut chicken breast into small pieces and set aside
2. In a pan heat olive oil and cook the chicken breast for 4-5 minutes
3. In another bowl combine mayonnaise, curry powder and add mixture to the chicken
4. Add remaining ingredients and cook for another 10-12 minutes or until the chicken is ready
5. When ready remove from the pot and serve with white rice

Serves: *2*

Prep Time: *10*   Minutes

Cook Time: *50*   Minutes

Total Time: *60*   Minutes

INGREDIENTS

- 1 carrot
- 2 sweet potatoes
- 1 butternut squash
- 2 parsnips
- 1 rosemary spring
- 2 bay leaves

DIRECTIONS

1. Chop the vegetables into thin slices
2. Place everything in a prepare baking dish
3. Bake at 350 F for 40-45 minutes or until vegetables are golden brown
4. When ready remove from the oven and serve

Serves: *6-8*

Prep Time: *10*   Minutes

Cook Time: *15*   Minutes

Total Time: *25*   Minutes

INGREDIENTS

- 2 pork sausages
- 1 tablespoon olive oil
- 2 garlic cloves
- 1 tsp fennel seeds
- ½ lb. ricotta
- 1 cup mozzarella cheese
- 1 oz. parmesan cheese
- 1 pizza crust

DIRECTIONS

1. Spread tomato sauce on the pizza crust
2. Place all the toppings on the pizza crust
3. Bake the pizza at 425 F for 12-15 minutes
4. When ready remove pizza from the oven and serve

Serves: *6-8*
Prep Time: *10*   Minutes

Cook Time: *15*   Minutes

Total Time: *25*   Minutes

INGREDIENTS

- 1 pizza crust
- 1 tablespoon olive oil
- 1 garlic clove
- 1 cup tomatoes
- 1 cup mozzarella cheese
- 1 carrot
- 1 cucumber

DIRECTIONS

1. Spread tomato sauce on the pizza crust
2. Place all the toppings on the pizza crust
3. Bake the pizza at 425 F for 12-15 minutes
4. When ready remove pizza from the oven and serve

Serves: *1*

Prep Time: *5*   Minutes

Cook Time: *5*   Minutes

Total Time: *10* Minutes

INGREDIENTS

- 1 cabbage
- 1 bunch of baby carrots
- ½ cucumber
- 1 bun of cilantro
- 1 bunch of basil
- 1 onion

DIRECTIONS

1. **In a bowl combine all ingredients together and mix well**
2. **Serve with dressing**

EDAMAME FRITATTA

Serves: **2**

Prep Time: **10** Minutes

Cook Time: **20** Minutes

Total Time: **30** Minutes

INGREDIENTS

- 1 cup edamame
- 1 tablespoon olive oil
- ½ red onion
- 2 eggs
- ¼ tsp salt
- 2 oz. cheddar cheese
- 1 garlic clove
- ¼ tsp dill

DIRECTIONS

1. In a bowl whisk eggs with salt and cheese
2. In a frying pan heat olive oil and pour egg mixture
3. Add remaining ingredients and mix well
4. Serve when ready

Serves: *2*
Prep Time: *10* Minutes

Cook Time: *20* Minutes

Total Time: *30* Minutes

INGREDIENTS

- 1 tablespoon olive oil
- ½ red onion
- 2 eggs
- ¼ tsp salt
- 2 oz. cheddar cheese
- 1 garlic clove
- ¼ tsp dill

DIRECTIONS

1. In a bowl whisk eggs with salt and cheese
2. In a frying pan heat olive oil and pour egg mixture
3. Add remaining ingredients and mix well
4. Serve when ready

Serves: *2*

Prep Time: *10*   Minutes

Cook Time: *20*   Minutes

Total Time: *30*   Minutes

INGREDIENTS

- ½ lb. leaf
- 1 tablespoon olive oil
- ½ red onion
- 2 eggs
- ¼ tsp salt
- 2 oz. cheddar cheese
- 1 garlic clove
- ¼ tsp dill

DIRECTIONS

1. In a bowl whisk eggs with salt and cheese
2. In a frying pan heat olive oil and pour egg mixture
3. Add remaining ingredients and mix well
4. Serve when ready

Serves: **2**

Prep Time: **10**   Minutes

Cook Time: **20**   Minutes

Total Time: **30**   Minutes

INGREDIENTS

- 1 cup kale
- 1 tablespoon olive oil
- ½ red onion
- 2 eggs
- ¼ tsp salt
- 2 oz. cheddar cheese
- 1 garlic clove
- ¼ tsp dill

DIRECTIONS

1. **In a skillet sauté kale until tender**
2. **In a bowl whisk eggs with salt and cheese**
3. **In a frying pan heat olive oil and pour egg mixture**
4. **Add remaining ingredients and mix well**
5. **When ready serve with sautéed kale**

Serves: 2

Prep Time: **10**   Minutes

Cook Time: **20**   Minutes

Total Time: **30**   Minutes

INGREDIENTS

- ½ cup jicama
- 1 tablespoon olive oil
- ½ red onion
- 2 eggs
- ¼ tsp salt
- 2 oz. parmesan cheese
- 1 garlic clove
- ¼ tsp dill

DIRECTIONS

1. In a bowl whisk eggs with salt and parmesan cheese
2. In a frying pan heat olive oil and pour egg mixture
3. Add remaining ingredients and mix well
4. Serve when ready

BROCCOLI FRITATTA

Serves: *2*

Prep Time: *10*   Minutes

Cook Time: *20*   Minutes

Total Time: *30*   Minutes

INGREDIENTS

- 1 cup broccoli
- 1 tablespoon olive oil
- ½ red onion
- 2 eggs
- ¼ tsp salt
- 2 oz. cheddar cheese
- 1 garlic clove
- ¼ tsp dill

DIRECTIONS

1. In a skillet sauté broccoli until tender
2. In a bowl whisk eggs with salt and cheese
3. In a frying pan heat olive oil and pour egg mixture
4. Add remaining ingredients and mix well
5. When ready serve with sautéed broccoli

CAULIFLOWER SANDWICH

Serves: **2**

Prep Time: **10** Minutes

Cook Time: **30** Minutes

Total Time: **40** Minutes

INGREDIENTS

- 1 head cauliflower
- 4 tablespoons olive oil
- ¼ tsp salt
- ½ red onion
- 2 tablespoons tahini
- 1 clove garlic
- 4 slices gluten-free bread
- 1 avocado

DIRECTIONS

1. Toss the cauliflower with olive oil and roast at 400 F for 22-25 minutes
2. In a saucepan sauté the onion until soft
3. Add roasted cauliflower, tahini, olive oil, salt and cook for 1-2 minutes
4. Place everything in a blender and blend until smooth
5. Spread mixture over bread slices

Serves: *2*

Prep Time: *10* Minutes

Cook Time: *10* Minutes

Total Time: *20* Minutes

INGREDIENTS

- 1 can chickpeas
- ¼ red onion
- ¼ tsp turmeric
- 1 tablespoon dill
- ½ tsp garlic powder
- 1 tablespoon mustard
- ½ cup tahini
- 2 avocados

DIRECTIONS

1. Cut avocado in half and scoop out part of the interior
2. In a bowl combine together chickpeas with onion, turmeric, dill, garlic, tahini and mustard
3. Mix well and spoon mixture into avocado halves
4. Serve when ready

Serves: *2*

Prep Time: *10*   Minutes

Cook Time: *20*   Minutes

Total Time: *30*   Minutes

INGREDIENTS

- 2 cups kernels
- 1 tablespoon butter
- 1 jalapeno pepper
- 1 tsp chili powder
- 1 red onion
- ½ cup mayonnaise
- 1 tablespoon lime juice
- 2 tablespoons cilantro

DIRECTIONS

1. In a skillet melt butter over medium heat
2. Add corn and cook for 5-6 minutes
3. Add chili powder, jalapeno, red onion and cook on low heat
4. Add lime juice, mayonnaise and cook for another 2-3 minutes
5. Remove from heat, stir in cilantro and serve with tortilla chips

LEEK QUICHE

Serves: *4*

Prep Time: *10*   Minutes

Cook Time: *50*   Minutes

Total Time: *60*   Minutes

INGREDIENTS

- 1 tablespoon butter
- 1 bunch asparagus
- 1 leek
- ¼ tsp salt
- 2 eggs
- ½ cup vanilla yogurt
- 1 cup almond milk
- 1 cup cheese
- 1 pie crust

DIRECTIONS

1. In a saucepan melt butter, add leek, asparagus, pepper, salt and cook until vegetables are soft
2. In a bowl combine eggs, milk, yogurt and mix well
3. Place egg mixture on the pie crust
4. Top with asparagus and leek
5. Bake at 375 F for 40-45 minutes, when ready remove and serve

Serves: *3-4*

Prep Time: *10*   Minutes

Cook Time: *20*   Minutes

Total Time: *30*   Minutes

INGREDIENTS

- 2 delicata squashes
- 2 tablespoons olive oil
- 1 tsp curry powder
- 1 tsp salt

DIRECTIONS

1. Preheat the oven to 400 F
2. Cut everything in half lengthwise
3. Toss everything with olive oil and place onto a prepared baking sheet
4. Roast for 18-20 minutes at 400 F or until golden brown
5. When ready remove from the oven and serve

Serves: *2*

Prep Time: *10*   Minutes

Cook Time: *20*   Minutes

Total Time: *30*   Minutes

INGREDIENTS

- 1 lb. brussels sprouts
- 1 tablespoon olive oil
- 1 tablespoon parmesan cheese
- 1 tsp garlic powder
- 1 tsp seasoning

DIRECTIONS

1. Preheat the oven to 425 F
2. In a bowl toss everything with olive oil and seasoning
3. Spread everything onto a prepared baking sheet
4. Bake for 8-10 minutes or until crisp
5. When ready remove from the oven and serve

Serves: *2*

Prep Time: *10*   Minutes

Cook Time: *20*   Minutes

Total Time: *30*   Minutes

INGREDIENTS

- 1 lb. cucumber
- 1 tsp salt
- 1 tsp smoked paprika
- 1 tablespoon olive oil

DIRECTIONS

1. Preheat the oven to 425 F
2. In a bowl toss everything with olive oil and seasoning
3. Spread everything onto a prepared baking sheet
4. Bake for 8-10 minutes or until crisp
5. When ready remove from the oven and serve

Serves: **2**

Prep Time: **10** Minutes

Cook Time: **20** Minutes

Total Time: **30** Minutes

INGREDIENTS

- 1 lb. squash
- 1 tsp salt
- 1 tsp smoked paprika
- 1 tablespoon olive oil

DIRECTIONS

1. Preheat the oven to 425 F
2. In a bowl toss everything with olive oil and seasoning
3. Spread everything onto a prepared baking sheet
4. Bake for 8-10 minutes or until crisp
5. When ready remove from the oven and serve

SIMPLE SPAGHETTI

Serves: *2*
Prep Time: *5*   Minutes

Cook Time: *15*   Minutes

Total Time: *20*   Minutes

INGREDIENTS

- 10 oz. spaghetti
- 2 eggs
- ½ cup parmesan cheese
- 1 tsp black pepper
- Olive oil
- 1 tsp parsley
- 2 cloves garlic

DIRECTIONS

1. In a pot boil spaghetti (or any other type of pasta), drain and set aside
2. In a bowl whish eggs with parmesan cheese
3. In a skillet heat olive oil, add garlic and cook for 1-2 minutes
4. Pour egg mixture and mix well
5. Add pasta and stir well

6. When ready garnish with parsley and serve

Serves: *2*

Prep Time: *5*   Minutes

Cook Time: *15*   Minutes

Total Time: *20*   Minutes

INGREDIENTS

- ¼ cup mayonnaise
- ¼ cup sweet chili sauce
- 1 tablespoon lime juice
- 1 garlic clove
- 8 z. pasta
- 1 lb. shrimp
- ¼ tsp paprika

DIRECTIONS

1. In a pot boil spaghetti (or any other type of pasta), drain and set aside
2. Place all the ingredients for the sauce in a pot and bring to a simmer
3. Add pasta and mix well
4. When ready garnish with parmesan cheese and serve

Serves: 2
Prep Time: 5   Minutes

Cook Time: 15   Minutes

Total Time: 20   Minutes

INGREDIENTS

- 8 oz. pasta
- 3 tablespoons olive oil
- 2 cloves garlic
- 5-6 anchovy fillets
- 2 cups tomatoes
- 1 cup olives
- ½ cup basil leaves

DIRECTIONS

1. In a pot boil spaghetti (or any other type of pasta), drain and set aside
2. Place all the ingredients for the sauce in a pot and bring to a simmer
3. Add pasta and mix well
4. When ready garnish with parmesan cheese and serve

MORNING SALAD

Serves: **2**

Prep Time: **5**   Minutes

Cook Time: **5**   Minutes

Total Time: **10**   Minutes

INGREDIENTS

- 1 onion
- 1 tsp cumin
- 1 tablespoon olive oil
- 1 avocado
- ¼ lb. cooked lentils
- 1 oz. walnuts
- Coriander
- ¼ lb. feta cheese
- Salad dressing of choice
- 8-10 baby carrots

DIRECTIONS

1. In a bowl combine all ingredients together and mix well
2. Add dressing and serve

Serves: *1*

Prep Time: 5   Minutes

Cook Time: **10**   Minutes

Total Time: **15**   Minutes

INGREDIENTS

- ¾ cup chicken broth
- 2 tbs tomato paste
- 2 tbs milk
- ½ cup tomatoes
- 1 tbs vinegar
- 1 tbs onion
- 1 clove garlic
- 1 tsp oregano
- Salt
- Pepper
- Basil leaves

DIRECTIONS

1. Pulse the ingredients in a food processor, saving the basil for garnish.
2. Cook the mixture until heated.
3. Serve garnished with basil leaves and toast.

CRAB SALAD

Serves: *1*

Prep Time: *5*   Minutes

Cook Time: *10*   Minutes

Total Time: *15*   Minutes

INGREDIENTS

- ½ cup celery
- 1 tbs vinegar
- 1 tsp seasoning
- 100 g crab
- Red pepper flakes
- 2 tbs lemon juice
- 2 tbs onion

DIRECTIONS

1. Sauté the ingredients in a pan until celery is tender.
2. Season to taste.
3. Serve when ready

45

Serves: *1*

Prep Time: 5   Minutes

Cook Time: 5   Minutes

Total Time: *10*   Minutes

INGREDIENTS

- ½ cup orange segments
- 1 packet stevia
- 1 toast
- 100g chicken breast
- ¼ tsp salt
- Orange citrus dressing
- 2 cups romaine lettuce

DIRECTIONS

1. Cook the chicken in a skillet until golden.
2. Combine all of the ingredients in a bowl.
3. Serve immediately.

Serves: *1*

Prep Time: 5   Minutes

Cook Time: *10*   Minutes

Total Time: *15*   Minutes

INGREDIENTS

- 100g chicken
- ½ tsp onion powder
- ½ tsp garlic powder
- ½ tsp oregano
- 1 tsp paprika
- ½ tsp thyme
- ½ tsp black pepper
- ¼ tsp salad greens

DIRECTIONS

1. Rub the chicken with the combined spices.
2. Grill the pink until golden.
3. Serve over the salad greens and desired dressing.

Serves: *1*

Prep Time: *5* Minutes

Cook Time: *0* Minutes

Total Time: *5* Minutes

INGREDIENTS

- ¼ tsp salt
- 2 tsp parsley
- ¼ cup vinegar
- 2 tsp green onion
- Pepper
- Stevia
- 1 cucumber

DIRECTIONS

1. Chop the cucumber.
2. Mix the ingredients in a bowl.
3. Refrigerate for at least 10 minutes, then serve.

Serves: *1*

Prep Time: *10*   Minutes

Cook Time: *0*   Minutes

Total Time: *10*   Minutes

INGREDIENTS

- 2 tbs apple vinegar
- Grapefruit juice
- ½ tsp ginger
- Salt
- 1 red grapefruit
- 1 cucumber
- Pepper
- Cilantro
- 2 tbs onion
- Ruby red dressing

DIRECTIONS

1. Peel the grapefruit and cut it into cubes.
2. Mix with the rest of the ingredients and season.
3. Serve topped with red dressing.

Serves: 2

Prep Time: 5   Minutes

Cook Time: 0   Minutes

Total Time: 5   Minutes

INGREDIENTS

- ½ cup green apple
- 1 tbs lemon juice
- Salt
- Pepper
- Stevia
- ½ cup cucumber
- 2 tbs apple cider vinegar

DIRECTIONS

1. Chop the apple and cucumber.
2. Combine the ingredients and add stevia.
3. Serve immediately.

Serves: *1*

Prep Time: *10*   Minutes

Cook Time: *0*   Minutes

Total Time: *10*   Minutes

INGREDIENTS

- 1 ½ cups cabbage
- ¼ tsp onion powder
- Cayenne pepper
- Salt
- Pepper
- 2 tbs vinegar
- 2 tbs lemon juice
- 1 tsp horseradish
- 1 clove garlic
- ½ tsp mustard

DIRECTIONS

1. Slice the cabbage.
2. Mix the rest of the ingredients in a bowl.
3. Pour the mixture over the cabbage and serve.

Serves: *1*

Prep Time: 5   Minutes

Cook Time: 5   Minutes

Total Time: *10*   Minutes

INGREDIENTS

- 100g lobster
- 1 serving Tarragon Vinaigrette
- 2 tbs lemon juice
- 1 tbs tarragon
- ½ tsp garlic powder
- 2 tbs onion
- 1 tbs green onion

DIRECTIONS

1. Cook the lobster.
2. Sauté the lobster, lemon juice, green onion, onion, tarragon, garlic powder, salt, and pepper until onion is tender.
3. Top the lettuce with the lobster mixture.
4. Serve topped with Tarragon Vinaigrette.

Serves: *1*

Prep Time: *10* Minutes

Cook Time: *20* Minutes

Total Time: *30* Minutes

INGREDIENTS

- 2 tbs lemon juice
- 1 tbs onion
- 1 tbs parsley
- Salt
- Radishes
- Pepper

DIRECTIONS

1. Combine all of the ingredients in a bowl.
2. Refrigerate for at least 20 minutes.
3. Serve.

Serves: **1**

Prep Time: **5** Minutes

Cook Time: **5** Minutes

Total Time: **10** Minutes

INGREDIENTS

- 1 bunch spinach
- Pepper
- Mint leaves
- 2 tbs vinegar
- 2 tbs lemon juice
- 5 strawberries
- ¼ tsp Stevia
- Salt

DIRECTIONS

1. Blend 2 strawberries, lemon juice, vinegar, Stevia, salt, and pepper together.
2. Pour the dressing over the salad and the sliced remained strawberry.
3. Serve topped with mint leaves.

SECOND COOKBOOK

BEANS OMELETTE

Serves: *1*

Prep Time: 5   Minutes

Cook Time: *10*   Minutes

Total Time: *15*   Minutes

INGREDIENTS

- 2 eggs
- ¼ tsp salt
- ¼ tsp black pepper
- 1 tablespoon olive oil
- ¼ cup cheese
- ¼ tsp basil
- 1 cup beans

DIRECTIONS

1. In a bowl combine all ingredients together and mix well
2. In a skillet heat olive oil and pour the egg mixture
3. Cook for 1-2 minutes per side
4. When ready remove omelette from the skillet and serve

Serves: *1*

Prep Time: *5*   Minutes

Cook Time: *10*   Minutes

Total Time: *15*   Minutes

INGREDIENTS

- 2 eggs
- ¼ tsp salt
- ¼ tsp black pepper
- 1 tablespoon olive oil
- ¼ cup cheese
- ¼ tsp basil
- 1 cup Asian greens

DIRECTIONS

1. In a bowl combine all ingredients together and mix well
2. In a skillet heat olive oil and pour the egg mixture
3. Cook for 1-2 minutes per side
4. When ready remove omelette from the skillet and serve

Serves: *1*

Prep Time: *5*   Minutes

Cook Time: **10**   Minutes

Total Time: **15**   Minutes

INGREDIENTS

- 2 eggs
- ¼ tsp salt
- ¼ tsp black pepper
- 1 tablespoon olive oil
- ¼ cup cheese
- ¼ tsp basil
- 1 cup beans

DIRECTIONS

1. In a bowl combine all ingredients together and mix well
2. In a skillet heat olive oil and pour the egg mixture
3. Cook for 1-2 minutes per side
4. When ready remove omelette from the skillet and serve

Serves: *1*
Prep Time: *5*   Minutes

Cook Time: *10*   Minutes

Total Time: *15*   Minutes

INGREDIENTS

- 2 eggs
- ¼ tsp salt
- ¼ tsp black pepper
- 1 tablespoon olive oil
- ¼ cup cheese
- ¼ tsp basil
- 1 cup red onion
- 1 cup cabbage

DIRECTIONS

1. In a bowl combine all ingredients together and mix well
2. In a skillet heat olive oil and pour the egg mixture
3. Cook for 1-2 minutes per side
4. When ready remove omelette from the skillet and serve

MUSHROOM OMELETTE

Serves: *1*

Prep Time: 5 Minutes

Cook Time: *10* Minutes

Total Time: *15* Minutes

INGREDIENTS

- 2 eggs
- ¼ tsp salt
- ¼ tsp black pepper
- 1 tablespoon olive oil
- ¼ cup cheese
- ¼ tsp basil
- 1 cup mushrooms

DIRECTIONS

1. In a bowl combine all ingredients together and mix well
2. In a skillet heat olive oil and pour the egg mixture
3. Cook for 1-2 minutes per side
4. When ready remove omelette from the skillet and serve

Serves: *1*

Prep Time: *5* Minutes

Cook Time: *10* Minutes

Total Time: *15* Minutes

INGREDIENTS

- 2 eggs
- ¼ tsp salt
- ¼ tsp black pepper
- 1 tablespoon olive oil
- ¼ cup cheese
- ¼ tsp basil
- 1 cup tomatoes

DIRECTIONS

1. In a bowl combine all ingredients together and mix well
2. In a skillet heat olive oil and pour the egg mixture
3. Cook for 1-2 minutes per side
4. When ready remove omelette from the skillet and serve

Serves: *1*

Prep Time: **5**   Minutes

Cook Time: **5**   Minutes

Total Time: ***10***   Minutes

INGREDIENTS

- 1 cup oats
- 3 tablespoons peanut butter
- ½ cup almond milk
- ¼ banana

DIRECTIONS

1. In a bowl combine all ingredients together and mix well
2. Pour mixture into a jar
3. Refrigerate overnight
4. Serve in the morning

Serves: 2

Prep Time: 5   Minutes

Cook Time: *30*   Minutes

Total Time: *35*   Minutes

INGREDIENTS

- 1 tsp vanilla extract
- 1 tablespoon honey
- 1 lb. rolled oats
- 2 tablespoons sesame seeds
- ¼ lb. almonds
- ¼ lb. berries

DIRECTIONS

1. Preheat the oven to 325 F
2. Spread the granola onto a baking sheet
3. Bake for 12-15 minutes, remove and mix everything
4. Bake for another 12-15 minutes or until slightly brown
5. When ready remove from the oven and serve

63

Serves:	*4*
Prep Time:	*10* Minutes
Cook Time:	*20* Minutes
Total Time:	*30* Minutes

INGREDIENTS

- 1 cup whole wheat flour
- ¼ tsp baking soda
- ¼ tsp baking powder
- 1 cup mashed banana
- 2 eggs
- 1 cup milk

DIRECTIONS

1. In a bowl combine all ingredients together and mix well
2. In a skillet heat olive oil
3. Pour ¼ of the batter and cook each pancake for 1-2 minutes per side
4. When ready remove from heat and serve

Serves: **4**

Prep Time: **10**   Minutes

Cook Time: **20**   Minutes

Total Time: **30**   Minutes

INGREDIENTS

- 1 cup whole wheat flour
- ¼ tsp baking soda
- ¼ tsp baking powder
- 1 cup lime
- 2 eggs
- 1 cup milk

DIRECTIONS

1. In a bowl combine all ingredients together and mix well
2. In a skillet heat olive oil
3. Pour ¼ of the batter and cook each pancake for 1-2 minutes per side
4. When ready remove from heat and serve

Serves: *4*

Prep Time: *10*   Minutes

Cook Time: *30*   Minutes

Total Time: *40*   Minutes

INGREDIENTS

- 1 cup whole wheat flour
- ¼ tsp baking soda
- ¼ tsp baking powder
- 2 eggs
- 1 cup milk
- 1 cup guava

DIRECTIONS

1. In a bowl combine all ingredients together and mix well
2. In a skillet heat olive oil
3. Pour ¼ of the batter and cook each pancake for 1-2 minutes per side
4. When ready remove from heat and serve

APRICOT MUFFINS

Serves: **8-12**

Prep Time: **10** Minutes

Cook Time: **20** Minutes

Total Time: **30** Minutes

INGREDIENTS

- 2 eggs
- 1 tablespoon olive oil
- 1 cup milk
- 2 cups whole wheat flour
- 1 tsp baking soda
- ¼ tsp baking soda
- 1 tsp ginger
- 1 cup apricot
- ¼ cup molasses

DIRECTIONS

1. In a bowl combine all dry ingredients
2. In another bowl combine all dry ingredients
3. Combine wet and dry ingredients together
4. Pour mixture into 8-12 prepared muffin cups, fill 2/3 of the cups
5. Bake for 18-20 minutes at 375 F, when ready remove and serve

PEACH MUFFINS

Serves: *8-12*

Prep Time: *10*   Minutes

Cook Time: *20*   Minutes

Total Time: *30*   Minutes

INGREDIENTS

- 2 eggs
- 1 tablespoon olive oil
- 1 cup milk
- 2 cups whole wheat flour
- 1 tsp baking soda
- ¼ tsp baking soda
- 1 tsp cinnamon
- 1 cup mashed peaches

DIRECTIONS

1. In a bowl combine all dry ingredients
2. In another bowl combine all dry ingredients
3. Combine wet and dry ingredients together
4. Pour mixture into 8-12 prepared muffin cups, fill 2/3 of the cups
5. Bake for 18-20 minutes at 375 F
6. When ready remove from the oven and serve

BLUEBERRY MUFFINS

Serves: *8-12*

Prep Time: *10*   Minutes

Cook Time: *20*   Minutes

Total Time: *30*   Minutes

INGREDIENTS

- 2 eggs
- 1 tablespoon olive oil
- 1 cup milk
- 2 cups whole wheat flour
- 1 tsp baking soda
- ¼ tsp baking soda
- 1 tsp cinnamon
- 1 cup blueberries

DIRECTIONS

1. In a bowl combine all dry ingredients
2. In another bowl combine all dry ingredients
3. Combine wet and dry ingredients together
4. Fold in blueberries and mix well
5. Pour mixture into 8-12 prepared muffin cups, fill 2/3 of the cups
6. Bake for 18-20 minutes at 375 F, when ready remove and serve

Serves: *8-12*

Prep Time: *10*   Minutes

Cook Time: *20*   Minutes

Total Time: *30*   Minutes

INGREDIENTS

- 2 eggs
- 1 tablespoon olive oil
- 1 cup milk
- 2 cups whole wheat flour
- 1 tsp baking soda
- ¼ tsp baking soda
- 1 tsp cinnamon
- 1 cup papaya

DIRECTIONS

1. In a bowl combine all dry ingredients
2. In another bowl combine all dry ingredients
3. Combine wet and dry ingredients together
4. Pour mixture into 8-12 prepared muffin cups, fill 2/3 of the cups
5. Bake for 18-20 minutes at 375 F
6. When ready remove from the oven and serve

Serves: *1*

Prep Time: *5*   Minutes

Cook Time: *10*   Minutes

Total Time: *15*   Minutes

INGREDIENTS

- 2 eggs
- ¼ tsp salt
- ¼ tsp black pepper
- 1 tablespoon olive oil
- ¼ cup cheese
- ¼ tsp basil
- 1 cup corn

DIRECTIONS

1. In a bowl combine all ingredients together and mix well
2. In a skillet heat olive oil and pour the egg mixture
3. Cook for 1-2 minutes per side
4. When ready remove omelette from the skillet and serve

Serves: **1**

Prep Time: **5** Minutes

Cook Time: **10** Minutes

Total Time: **15** Minutes

INGREDIENTS

- 2 eggs
- ¼ tsp salt
- ¼ tsp black pepper
- 1 tablespoon olive oil
- ¼ cup cheese
- ¼ tsp basil
- 1 cup mushrooms

DIRECTIONS

1. In a bowl combine all ingredients together and mix well
2. In a skillet heat olive oil and pour the egg mixture
3. Cook for 1-2 minutes per side
4. When ready remove omelette from the skillet and serve

YAMS OMELETTE

Serves: *1*

Prep Time: **5**   Minutes

Cook Time: **10**   Minutes

Total Time: **15**   Minutes

INGREDIENTS

- 2 eggs
- ¼ tsp salt
- ¼ tsp black pepper
- 1 tablespoon olive oil
- ¼ cup cheese
- ¼ tsp basil
- 1 cup yams

DIRECTIONS

1. In a bowl combine all ingredients together and mix well
2. In a skillet heat olive oil and pour the egg mixture
3. Cook for 1-2 minutes per side
4. When ready remove omelette from the skillet and serve

73

Serves: *1*

Prep Time: *5* Minutes

Cook Time: *5* Minutes

Total Time: *10* Minutes

INGREDIENTS

- ½ cup dried raisins
- ½ cup dried pecans
- ¼ cup almonds
- 1 cup coconut milk
- 1 tsp cinnamon

DIRECTIONS

1. In a bowl combine all ingredients together
2. Serve with milk

Serves: 2
Prep Time: 5   Minutes

Cook Time: *15*   Minutes

Total Time: *20*   Minutes

INGREDIENTS

- ¼ cup egg substitute
- 1 muffin
- 1 turkey sausage patty
- 1 tablespoon cheddar cheese

DIRECTIONS

1. In a skillet pour egg and cook on low heat
2. Place turkey sausage patty in a pan and cook for 4-5 minutes per side
3. On a toasted muffin place the cooked egg, top with a sausage patty and cheddar cheese
4. Serve when ready

Serves: *8-12*

Prep Time: *10*   Minutes

Cook Time: *20*   Minutes

Total Time: *30*   Minutes

INGREDIENTS

- 2 eggs
- 1 tablespoon olive oil
- 1 cup milk
- 2 cups whole wheat flour
- 1 tsp baking soda
- ¼ tsp baking soda
- 1 tsp cinnamon
- 1 cup strawberries

DIRECTIONS

1. In a bowl combine all dry ingredients
2. In another bowl combine all dry ingredients
3. Combine wet and dry ingredients together
4. Pour mixture into 8-12 prepared muffin cups, fill 2/3 of the cups
5. Bake for 18-20 minutes at 375 F
6. When ready remove from the oven and serve

Serves: *2*

Prep Time: *10*   Minutes

Cook Time: *20*   Minutes

Total Time: *30*   Minutes

INGREDIENTS

- ½ lb. leek
- 1 tablespoon olive oil
- ½ red onion
- ¼ tsp salt
- 2 ggs
- 2 oz. cheddar cheese
- 1 garlic clove
- ¼ tsp dill

DIRECTIONS

1. In a bowl whisk eggs with salt and cheese
2. In a frying pan heat olive oil and pour egg mixture
3. Add remaining ingredients and mix well
4. Serve when ready

KALE FRITATTA

Serves: *2*

Prep Time: *10* Minutes

Cook Time: *20* Minutes

Total Time: *30* Minutes

INGREDIENTS

- 1 cup kale
- 1 tablespoon olive oil
- ½ red onion
- ¼ tsp salt
- 2 eggs
- 2 oz. cheddar cheese
- 1 garlic clove
- ¼ tsp dill

DIRECTIONS

1. In a skillet sauté kale until tender
2. In a bowl whisk eggs with salt and cheese
3. In a frying pan heat olive oil and pour egg mixture
4. Add remaining ingredients and mix well
5. Serve when ready

GREENS FRITATTA

Serves: **2**
Prep Time: **10** Minutes

Cook Time: **20** Minutes

Total Time: **30** Minutes

INGREDIENTS

- ½ lb. greens
- 1 tablespoon olive oil
- ½ red onion
- ¼ tsp salt
- 2 eggs
- 2 oz. parmesan cheese
- 1 garlic clove
- ¼ tsp dill

DIRECTIONS

1. In a bowl whisk eggs with salt and parmesan cheese
2. In a frying pan heat olive oil and pour egg mixture
3. Add remaining ingredients and mix well
4. Serve when ready

Serves: **2**

Prep Time: **10** Minutes

Cook Time: **20** Minutes

Total Time: **30** Minutes

INGREDIENTS

- 1 cup broccoli
- 1 tablespoon olive oil
- ½ red onion
- ¼ tsp salt
- 2 oz. cheddar cheese
- 1 garlic clove
- ¼ tsp dill

DIRECTIONS

1. In a skillet sauté broccoli until tender
2. In a bowl whisk eggs with salt and cheese
3. In a frying pan heat olive oil and pour egg mixture
4. Add remaining ingredients and mix well
5. When ready serve with sautéed broccoli

BREAKFAST COOKIES

Serves: *8-12*

Prep Time: 5   Minutes

Cook Time: *15*   Minutes

Total Time: *20*   Minutes

INGREDIENTS

- 1 cup rolled oats
- ¼ cup applesauce
- ½ tsp vanilla extract
- 3 tablespoons chocolate chips
- 2 tablespoons dried fruits
- 1 tsp cinnamon

DIRECTIONS

1. Preheat the oven to 325 F
2. In a bowl combine all ingredients together and mix well
3. Scoop cookies using an ice cream scoop
4. Place cookies onto a prepared baking sheet
5. Place in the oven for 12-15 minutes or until the cookies are done
6. When ready remove from the oven and serve

Serves: *8-12*
Prep Time: *15*   Minutes

Cook Time: *35*   Minutes

Total Time: *50*   Minutes

INGREDIENTS

- pastry sheets
- ¼ tsp lavender
- 1 cup brown sugar
- 4-5 cups blueberries
- 1 tablespoon lemon juice
- 1 cup almonds
- 2 tablespoons butter

DIRECTIONS

1. Line a pie plate or pie form with pastry and cover the edges of the plate depending on your preference
2. In a bowl combine all pie ingredients together and mix well
3. Pour the mixture over the pastry
4. Bake at 400-425 F for 25-30 minutes or until golden brown
5. When ready remove from the oven and let it rest for 15 minutes

Serves: *8-12*

Prep Time: *15*   Minutes

Cook Time: *35*   Minutes

Total Time: *50*   Minutes

INGREDIENTS

- pastry sheets
- 1 cup buttermilk
- 1 can pumpkin
- 1 cup sugar
- 1 tsp cinnamon
- 1 tsp vanilla extract
- 2 eggs

DIRECTIONS

1. Line a pie plate or pie form with pastry and cover the edges of the plate depending on your preference
2. In a bowl combine all pie ingredients together and mix well
3. Pour the mixture over the pastry
4. Bake at 400-425 F for 25-30 minutes or until golden brown
5. When ready remove from the oven and let it rest for 15 minutes

Serves: *6-8*

Prep Time: *15*   Minutes

Cook Time: *15*   Minutes

Total Time: *30*   Minutes

INGREDIENTS

- 1 cup almonds
- 1-pint vanilla ice cream
- 2 cups ricotta cheese
- 1 cup honey

DIRECTIONS

1. In a saucepan whisk together all ingredients
2. Mix until bubbly
3. Strain into a bowl and cool
4. Whisk in favorite fruits and mix well
5. Cover and refrigerate for 2-3 hours
6. Pour mixture in the ice-cream maker and follow manufacturer instructions
7. Serve when ready

Serves: *6-8*

Prep Time: *15*   Minutes

Cook Time: *15*   Minutes

Total Time: *30*   Minutes

INGREDIENTS

- 4 egg yolks
- 1 cup heavy cream
- 1 cup milk
- ½ cup brown sugar
- 1 tsp saffron
- 1 tsp vanilla extract

DIRECTIONS

1. In a saucepan whisk together all ingredients
2. Mix until bubbly
3. Strain into a bowl and cool
4. Whisk in favorite fruits and mix well
5. Cover and refrigerate for 2-3 hours
6. Pour mixture in the ice-cream maker and follow manufacturer instructions
7. Serve when ready

TURMERIC-MANGO SMOOTHIE

Serves:	*1*
Prep Time:	*5* Minutes
Cook Time:	*5* Minutes
Total Time:	*10* Minutes

INGREDIENTS

- 1 cup Greek yogurt
- ¼ cup orange juice
- 1 banana
- 1 tablespoon turmeric
- 1 tsp vanilla extract
- 1 cup ice

DIRECTIONS

1. In a blender place all ingredients and blend until smooth
2. Pour smoothie in a glass and serve

AVOCADO-KALE SMOOTHIE

Serves: *1*

Prep Time: **5**   Minutes

Cook Time: **5**   Minutes

Total Time: *10*   Minutes

INGREDIENTS

- 1 cup coconut milk
- 1 tablespoon lemon juice
- 1 bunch kale
- 1 cup spinach
- ¼ avocado
- 1 cup ice

DIRECTIONS

1. In a blender place all ingredients and blend until smooth
2. Pour smoothie in a glass and serve

Serves: *1*

Prep Time: 5   Minutes

Cook Time: 5   Minutes

Total Time: *10*   Minutes

INGREDIENTS

- 1 cup ice
- 1 cup strawberries
- 1 cup blueberries
- 1 cup buttermilk
- ½ tsp vanilla extract

DIRECTIONS

1. In a blender place all ingredients and blend until smooth
2. Pour smoothie in a glass and serve

Serves: *1*

Prep Time: 5   Minutes

Cook Time: 5   Minutes

Total Time: *10*   Minutes

INGREDIENTS

- 1 cup berries
- 1 cup baby spinach
- 1 tablespoon orange juice
- ¼ cup coconut water
- ½ cup Greek yogurt

DIRECTIONS

1. In a blender place all ingredients and blend until smooth
2. Pour smoothie in a glass and serve

Serves: *1*

Prep Time: *5*   Minutes

Cook Time: *5*   Minutes

Total Time: *10*   Minutes

INGREDIENTS

- 1 mango
- 1 cup vanilla yogurt
- 2 tablespoons honey
- 1 tablespoon lime juice
- 1 banana
- 1 can strawberries
- 1 kiwi

DIRECTIONS

1. In a blender place all ingredients and blend until smooth
2. Pour smoothie in a glass and serve

Serves: *1*

Prep Time: *5*   Minutes

Cook Time: *5*   Minutes

Total Time: *10*   Minutes

INGREDIENTS

- 2 cups mango
- 1 cup buttermilk
- 1 tsp vanilla extract
- 1 cup kiwi
- ½ cup coconut milk

DIRECTIONS

1. In a blender place all ingredients and blend until smooth
2. Pour smoothie in a glass and serve

Serves: *1*

Prep Time: *5*   Minutes

Cook Time: *5*   Minutes

Total Time: *10*   Minutes

INGREDIENTS

- 1 cup Greek yogurt
- 1 cup ice
- ¼ cup mango
- 1 orange
- 1 pinch cinnamon

DIRECTIONS

1. In a blender place all ingredients and blend until smooth
2. Pour smoothie in a glass and serve

FIG SMOOTHIE

92

Serves: *1*

Prep Time: 5   Minutes

Cook Time: 5   Minutes

Total Time: *10*   Minutes

INGREDIENTS

- 1 cup ice
- 1 cup vanilla yogurt
- 1 cup coconut milk
- 1 tsp honey
- 4 figs

DIRECTIONS

1. In a blender place all ingredients and blend until smooth
2. Pour smoothie in a glass and serve

Serves: *1*

Prep Time: 5   Minutes

Cook Time: 5   Minutes

Total Time: *10*   Minutes

INGREDIENTS

- 2 cups blueberries
- 1 cup pomegranate
- 1 tablespoon honey
- 1 cup Greek yogurt

DIRECTIONS

1. In a blender place all ingredients and blend until smooth
2. Pour smoothie in a glass and serve

94

Serves: *1*

Prep Time: 5 Minutes

Cook Time: 5 Minutes

Total Time: *10* Minutes

INGREDIENTS

- 1 cup kale
- 1 banana
- 1 cup almond milk
- 1 cup vanilla yogurt
- 1 tsp chia seeds
- ¼ tsp ginger

DIRECTIONS

1. In a blender place all ingredients and blend until smooth
2. Pour smoothie in a glass and serve

THIRD COOKBOOK

CAULIFLOWER SOUP

Serves: **4**

Prep Time: **10**   Minutes

Cook Time: **20**   Minutes

Total Time: **30**   Minutes

INGREDIENTS

- 1 tablespoon olive oil
- 1 lb. cauliflower
- ¼ red onion
- ½ cup all-purpose flour
- ¼ tsp salt
- ¼ tsp pepper
- 1 can vegetable broth
- 1 cup heavy cream

DIRECTIONS

1. In a saucepan heat olive oil and sauté cauliflower until tender
2. Add remaining ingredients to the saucepan and bring to a boil
3. When all the vegetables are tender transfer to a blender and blend until smooth
4. Pour soup into bowls, garnish with parsley and serve

Serves: **4**

Prep Time: **10** Minutes

Cook Time: **30** Minutes

Total Time: **40** Minutes

INGREDIENTS

- 2 tablespoons unsalted butter
- ½ cup minced onion
- ½ cup mushrooms
- 2 tablespoons all-purpose flour
- ¼ cup low sodium chicken broth
- ¼ cup almond milk
- pepper

DIRECTIONS

1. In a soup pot add all soup ingredients
2. Sauté for 5-6 minutes
3. Add water simmer for 20-30 minutes
4. Season with pepper
5. When ready, pour into bowls and serve

Serves: **4**

Prep Time: **10**   Minutes

Cook Time: **20**   Minutes

Total Time: **30**   Minutes

INGREDIENTS

- 1 tablespoon olive oil
- 1 lb. zucchini
- ¼ red onion
- ½ cup all-purpose flour
- ¼ tsp salt
- ¼ tsp pepper
- 1 can vegetable broth
- 1 cup heavy cream

DIRECTIONS

1. In a saucepan heat olive oil and sauté zucchini until tender
2. Add remaining ingredients to the saucepan and bring to a boil
3. When all the vegetables are tender transfer to a blender and blend until smooth
4. Pour soup into bowls, garnish with parsley and serve

Serves: **4**

Prep Time: **10** Minutes

Cook Time: **20** Minutes

Total Time: **30** Minutes

INGREDIENTS

- 1 tablespoon olive oil
- 1 lb. celery
- ¼ red onion
- ½ cup all-purpose flour
- ¼ tsp salt
- ¼ tsp pepper
- 1 can vegetable broth
- 1 cup heavy cream

DIRECTIONS

1. In a saucepan heat olive oil and sauté celery until tender
2. Add remaining ingredients to the saucepan and bring to a boil
3. When all the vegetables are tender transfer to a blender and blend until smooth
4. Pour soup into bowls, garnish with parsley and serve

Serves: *4*

Prep Time: *10*   Minutes

Cook Time: *20*   Minutes

Total Time: *30*   Minutes

INGREDIENTS

- 1 tablespoon olive oil
- 1 lb. carrots
- ¼ red onion
- ½ cup all-purpose flour
- ¼ tsp salt
- ¼ tsp pepper
- 1 can vegetable broth
- 1 cup heavy cream

DIRECTIONS

1. In a saucepan heat olive oil and sauté carrots until tender
2. Add remaining ingredients to the saucepan and bring to a boil
3. When all the vegetables are tender transfer to a blender and blend until smooth
4. Pour soup into bowls, garnish with parsley and serve

Serves: **4**

Prep Time: **10** Minutes

Cook Time: **20** Minutes

Total Time: **30** Minutes

INGREDIENTS

- 1 tablespoon olive oil
- 1 lb. cucumber
- ¼ red onion
- ½ cup all-purpose flour
- ¼ tsp salt
- ¼ tsp pepper
- 1 can vegetable broth
- 1 cup heavy cream

DIRECTIONS

1. In a saucepan heat olive oil and sauté cucumber until tender
2. Add remaining ingredients to the saucepan and bring to a boil
3. When all the vegetables are tender transfer to a blender and blend until smooth
4. Pour soup into bowls, garnish with parsley and serve

GOAT'S CHEESE RAREBIT

Serves: **4**

Prep Time: **10**   Minutes

Cook Time: **30**   Minutes

Total Time: **40**   Minutes

INGREDIENTS

- 1 oz. olive oil
- 150 ml soya milk
- 6 oz. goat cheese
- 1 oz. flour
- ½ tsp mustard
- pepper
- 1 egg yolk
- 4 bread slices

DIRECTIONS

1. In a saucepan add butter, cheese, soya milk and cook on low heat
2. Stir in flour and bring mixture to a boil
3. Remove from heat add mustard, pepper and whisk in the egg yolks
4. Toast the bread and spread mixture between the slices

5. Place on a grill and cook until golden brown

Serves: *2*
Prep Time: *10*   Minutes

Cook Time: *10*   Minutes

Total Time: *20*   Minutes

INGREDIENTS

- 7 oz. smoked mackerel fillets
- 2 onions
- 1 lemon
- 3 oz. cream cheese
- 1 tablespoon creamed horseradish
- pepper

DIRECTIONS

1. Cut mackerel into small chunks
2. In a bowl mix cream cheese, mackerel, creamed horseradish, onions and zest of 1 lemon
3. Mix with lemon juice and season with pepper and pate that should be ready

Serves: *4*

Prep Time: *10*   Minutes

Cook Time: *30*   Minutes

Total Time: *40*   Minutes

INGREDIENTS

- 7 oz. basil pesto
- 3 oz. cream cheese
- 3 oz. sour cream
- 2 tablespoons parmesan cheese

DIRECTIONS

1. In a bowl add cream cheese, pesto, sour cream and parmesan cheese
2. Mix well and serve when ready

Serves: 6

Prep Time: *10*   Minutes

Cook Time: *20*   Minutes

Total Time: *30*   Minutes

INGREDIENTS

- 1 cauliflower
- 500 ml milk
- 3 tablespoons flour
- 2 oz. butter
- 3 oz. cheddar cheese
- 2 tablespoons breadcrumbs

DIRECTIONS

1. Preheat the oven to 400 F
2. In a saucepan add cauliflower and cook for 5-8 minutes
3. Add milk, butter, flour and whisk until mixture boils
4. Stir in cheese and pour over the cauliflower
5. Scatter over the remaining cheese and breadcrumbs
6. Bake cauliflower cheese for 18-20 minutes

Serves: *4*

Prep Time: *10*   Minutes

Cook Time: *30*   Minutes

Total Time: *40*   Minutes

INGREDIENTS

- 2 tablespoons olive oil
- 1 onion
- 500 ml chicken stock
- 10 sage leaves
- 6 oz. Arborio rice
- 9 oz. pumpkin
- 2 oz. butter
- 1 pinch black pepper
- parmesan cheese

DIRECTIONS

1. In a saucepan add ½ chicken stock and cook on low heat, add sage, onion, rice and continue to simmer
2. Add pumpkin, remaining stock and cook until stock is absorbed and pumpkin is soft
3. Stir in butter, season with pepper and divide into 2-3 servings
4. Add grated cheese and serve

Serves: **2**

Prep Time: **5**   Minutes

Cook Time: **15**   Minutes

Total Time: **20**   Minutes

INGREDIENTS

- 4 oz. spaghetti
- 2 cups basil leaves
- 2 garlic cloves
- ¼ cup olive oil
- 2 tablespoons parmesan cheese
- ½ tsp black pepper

DIRECTIONS

1. Bring water to a boil and add pasta
2. In a blend add parmesan cheese, basil leaves, garlic and blend
3. Add olive oil, pepper and blend again
4. Pour pesto onto pasta and serve when ready

Serves: *4*

Prep Time: *10*   Minutes

Cook Time: *20*   Minutes

Total Time: *30*   Minutes

INGREDIENTS

- 1 lb. beef
- 1 garlic clove
- 1 chili
- 1 onion
- 1 oz. fresh basil
- 1 tablespoon soy sauce
- 1 tablespoon vegetable oil

DIRECTIONS

1. Fry garlic, chili and mince over medium heat
2. Add the rest of ingredients and cook for 18-20 minutes
3. Remove from heat and serve with rice

Serves: **4**

Prep Time: **10** Minutes

Cook Time: **30** Minutes

Total Time: **40** Minutes

INGREDIENTS

- 2 pork chops
- 1 tsp mustard
- 1 tsp oil
- 1 spring onion
- 1 clove garlic
- 1 tablespoon breadcrumbs
- 1 pinch dried hers

DIRECTIONS

1. Preheat the oven to 375 F
2. Spread the mustard over the pork chop
3. In a bowl add garlic, dried herbs, breadcrumbs, onions and mix well
4. Spread the herb mixture on top of each pork chop
5. Bake for 20-25 minutes
6. Remove and serve with boiled potatoes

Serves: *4*

Prep Time: *10*   Minutes

Cook Time: *20*   Minutes

Total Time: *30*   Minutes

INGREDIENTS

- 1 lb. minced beef
- 1 onion
- 1 pinch dried herb
- 1 pinch black pepper

DIRECTIONS

1. Preheat the grill to hot
2. In a bowl mix all ingredients together
3. Divide mixture into 4 portion and shape into patties
4. Grill for 5-6 minutes per side or until brown
5. Serve in a burger bun with potato fries

Serves: *4*
Prep Time: *10*   Minutes

Cook Time: *30*   Minutes

Total Time: *40*   Minutes

INGREDIENTS

- 1 lb. boneless fish fillets
- juice of 1 lemon
- 1 tablespoon unsalted butter
- 1 pinch rosemary

DIRECTIONS

1. Preheat the oven to 325 F
2. Place the fish in a shallow baking dish
3. In a bowl mix all remaining ingredients
4. Dot over fish fillets
5. Bake for 25 minutes or until fish is tender
6. Serve with vegetables

Serves: **4**

Prep Time: **10** Minutes

Cook Time: **15** Minutes

Total Time: **25** Minutes

INGREDIENTS

- ½ lb. couscous
- 500 ml water
- 2 tablespoons mint
- 2 teaspoons olive oil

DIRECTIONS

1. In a saucepan bring water to a boil
2. Add couscous and cover with a lid
3. Drizzle oil, mint and cook until soft
4. Season with black pepper and serve with baked fish

Serves: *8*

Prep Time: *10*   minutes

Cook Time: *20*   minutes

Total Time: *30*   minutes

INGREDIENTS

- 2 lbs fresh lean ground pork
- ½ teaspoon black pepper
- 1 teaspoon lemon juice
- ½ teaspoon ground sage
- ½ teaspoon marjoram
- 1 teaspoon paprika

DIRECTIONS

1. Combine all ingredients in a bowl and mix them
2. Add 2-3 tablespoons water to the pork mixture and mix
3. Form into 8 patties
4. Spray skillet with cooking spray
5. Sprinkle the patties with paprika
6. Cook until crispy brown
7. Remove excess fat
8. Cooked pork patties can be frozen for later if you want

Serves: 2

Prep Time: 5   Minutes

Cook Time: 5   Minutes

Total Time: **10**   Minutes

INGREDIENTS

- 2 lb. cooked red potatoes
- 1 tablespoon salt
- ¼ cup olive oil
- ¼ cup parsley
- ¼ cup green onions
- 1 tablespoon lemon juice
- 1 tsp mustard
- 2 stalks celery

DIRECTIONS

1. In a bowl mix all ingredients and mix well
2. Serve with dressing

Serves: **2**

Prep Time: **5**   Minutes

Cook Time: **5**   Minutes

Total Time: **10**   Minutes

INGREDIENTS

- 1 can black beans
- 1 can chickpeas
- 1 red onion
- 2 stalks celery
- 1 cucumber
- ½ cup parsley
- 1 tablespoon mint
- 2 cloves garlic

DIRECTIONS

1. In a bowl combine all ingredients together and mix well
2. Serve with dressing

Serves:	**2**
Prep Time:	**5** Minutes
Cook Time:	**5** Minutes
Total Time:	**10** Minutes

INGREDIENTS

- 1 bunch kale
- 1 apple
- 1 fennel
- 4 oz. feta cheese
- ½ cup cranberries
- 1 cup maple syrup salad dressing

DIRECTIONS

1. In a bowl combine all ingredients together and mix well
2. Serve with dressing

Serves: 2

Prep Time: 5   Minutes

Cook Time: 5   Minutes

Total Time: *10*   Minutes

INGREDIENTS

- 1 cup quinoa
- 1 cup tomatoes
- 1 cup baby spinach
- 1 tablespoon olive oil
- 1 cup lemon salad dressing

DIRECTIONS

1. In a bowl combine all ingredients together and mix well
2. Serve with dressing

Serves: 2

Prep Time: 5   Minutes

Cook Time: 5   Minutes

Total Time: *10*   Minutes

INGREDIENTS

- 1 cup cooked wild rice
- 1 tsp olive oil
- 6 oz. arugula
- ¼ cup basil
- ½ cup cranberries
- ½ cup goat cheese
- 1 cup lemon salad dressing

DIRECTIONS

1. In a bowl combine all ingredients together and mix well
2. Serve with dressing

Serves: 2
Prep Time: 5   Minutes

Cook Time: 5   Minutes

Total Time: *10*   Minutes

INGREDIENTS

- 1 bunch kale
- 1 cup cooked grains
- 2 carrots
- 1 radish
- 1 tablespoon pepitas
- 1 cup tahini dressing

DIRECTIONS

1. In a bowl combine all ingredients together and mix well
2. Serve with dressing

Serves: 2

Prep Time: 5   Minutes

Cook Time: 5   Minutes

Total Time: 10   Minutes

INGREDIENTS

- 1 head leaf lettuce
- 1 red bell pepper
- 2 mangoes
- 1 cup green onion
- ½ cup peanuts
- ½ cup cilantro
- 1 cup peanut dressing

DIRECTIONS

1. In a bowl combine all ingredients together and mix well
2. Serve with dressing

Serves: **2**

Prep Time: **5**   Minutes

Cook Time: **5**   Minutes

Total Time: **10**   Minutes

INGREDIENTS

- 2 lb. cooked white potatoes
- 2 tablespoons olive oil
- ½ cup parsley
- ½ cup green onion
- 1 tablespoon lemon juice
- 1 tsp mustard
- 2 cloves garlic
- 1 tsp black pepper
- 1 tsp oregano

DIRECTIONS

1. In a bowl combine all ingredients together and mix well
2. Serve with dressing

Serves: 2

Prep Time: 5   Minutes

Cook Time: 5   Minutes

Total Time: *10*   Minutes

INGREDIENTS

- 1 cup cooked quinoa
- 1 cup edamame
- 1 cup pepitas
- 1 beet
- 1 carrot
- 1 cup baby spinach
- 1 avocado
- 1 cup lemon salad dressing

DIRECTIONS

1. **In a bowl combine all ingredients together and mix well**
2. **Serve with dressing**

Serves: 2
Prep Time: 5   Minutes

Cook Time: 5   Minutes

Total Time: *10*   Minutes

INGREDIENTS

- 6 oz. greens
- 1 apple
- 1 cup cranberries
- ½ cup pepitas
- 3 oz. feta cheese

DIRECTIONS

1. In a bowl combine all ingredients together and mix well
2. Serve with dressing

Serves: **1**

Prep Time: **5** Minutes

Cook Time: **10** Minutes

Total Time: **15** Minutes

INGREDIENTS

- 3 oz. shrimp
- ¼ cup zucchini
- ½ cup fiesta garden salsa
- ¼ oz. cheese
- cilantro
- 1 tortilla

DIRECTIONS

1. In a bowl add zucchini, shrimp and pour salsa over
2. Microwave for 4-5 minutes and sprinkle with grated cheese and cilantro
3. Microwave tortilla for 10-20 seconds and serve with shrimp

CAULIFLOWER FRITTERS

Serves: *8*

Prep Time: *10*   Minutes

Cook Time: *30*   Minutes

Total Time: *40*   Minutes

INGREDIENTS

- 1 head of cauliflower
- ¼ tsp chili powder
- 2 cloves garlic
- 2 tablespoons cilantro
- 1 tsp salt
- ¼ tsp black pepper
- 2 eggs
- 3 tablespoons cornmeal
- ½ cup flour
- 4 tablespoons nutritional yeast

DIRECTIONS

1. Cook cauliflower florets by steaming for 5-6 minutes
2. Mix the cauliflower with chili powder, cilantro, garlic, pepper and salt
3. In another bowl beat the egg, add cauliflower mixture, flour, cornmeal, and yeast

4. Add ¼ cup of the mixture to the pan and press down the fritter
5. Cook until golden brown for 3-4 minutes per side
6. When ready, remove and serve

Serves: **2**

Prep Time: **5**   Minutes

Cook Time: **10**   Minutes

Total Time: **15**   Minutes

INGREDIENTS

- **4 thin slices bread**
- **2 eggs**
- **1/3 cup almond milk**
- **¼ tsp vanilla extract**
- **1 tablespoon cream cheese**
- **1 tablespoon apricot preserves**
- **½ cup maple syrup**

DIRECTIONS

1. **In a bowl combine vanilla extract, eggs, almond milk, and mix well**
2. **Make 2 sandwiches with cream cheese and preserve**
3. **Place sandwiches in egg mixture on both sides**
4. **In a skillet cook sandwiches for 2-3 minutes per side or until golden brown**
5. **When ready remove and serve**

Serves: *6*

Prep Time: *10*   Minutes

Cook Time: *90*   Minutes

Total Time: *100*   Minutes

INGREDIENTS

- ½ cup olive oil
- 1 eggplant
- 1 onion
- 2 garlic cloves
- 1 lb. potatoes
- 5 tomatoes
- 10 cherry tomatoes
- 1 cup tomato passata
- 1 cup water
- 1 tablespoon dried oregano
- 1 tablespoon parsley
- 1 tsp salt

DIRECTIONS

1. **Preheat the oven to 400 F**
2. **In a frying pan add olive oil, eggplant and cook for 6-7 minutes**

3. Add garlic, onion and sauté for 5-6 minutes

4. Add potato, zucchini, passata, tomatoes, and water

5. Sprinkle with oregano, parsley, pepper, and salt

6. Mix well and transfer to a baking dish, drizzle with olive oil and bake for 45-55 minutes or until the top has browned

7. When ready remove and serve

Serves: **4**

Prep Time: **5** Minutes

Cook Time: **15** Minutes

Total Time: **20** Minutes

INGREDIENTS

- 2 salmon steaks
- 2 tablespoons dipping sauce
- 1 tsp cooking oil

DIRECTIONS

1. Heat grill and rub with cooking oil
2. Baste steaks with sauce
3. Cook for 4-5 minutes per side
4. Don't overcook
5. When ready remove and serve

Serves: *8*
Prep Time: *10*   Minutes

Cook Time: *90*   Minutes

Total Time: *100*   Minutes

INGREDIENTS

- ¼ cup green beans
- ¼ cup snow peas
- 1 cup cauliflower florets
- 1 cup water chestnuts
- 2 radishes
- 2 scallions
- ½ cup red onion
- 1 tsp powdered ginger
- ½ cup rice wine vinegar

DIRECTIONS

1. In a bowl combine cauliflower floret, radish slices, onions, water chestnuts and mix well
2. In another bowl combine rice wine vinegar, powdered ginger and pour over vegetables
3. Refrigerate for 1-2 hours
4. When ready remove and serve

BROCCOLI CASSEROLE

Serves: *4*

Prep Time: *10*   Minutes

Cook Time: *15*   Minutes

Total Time: *25*   Minutes

INGREDIENTS

- 1 onion
- 2 chicken breasts
- 2 tablespoons unsalted butter
- 2 eggs
- 2 cups cooked rice
- 2 cups cheese
- 1 cup parmesan cheese
- 2 cups cooked broccoli

DIRECTIONS

1. Sauté the veggies and set aside
2. Preheat the oven to 425 F
3. Transfer the sautéed veggies to a baking dish, add remaining ingredients to the baking dish
4. Mix well, add seasoning and place the dish in the oven
5. Bake for 12-15 minutes or until slightly brown
6. When ready remove from the oven and serve

Serves: *2*

Prep Time: *10*   Minutes

Cook Time: *20*   Minutes

Total Time: *30*   Minutes

INGREDIENTS

- 1 cup black beans
- 1 tablespoon olive oil
- ½ red onion
- 2 eggs
- ¼ tsp salt
- 2 oz. cheddar cheese
- 1 garlic clove
- ¼ tsp dill

DIRECTIONS

1. In a bowl whisk eggs with salt and cheese
2. In a frying pan heat olive oil and pour egg mixture
3. Add remaining ingredients and mix well
4. Serve when ready

Serves: **3-4**

Prep Time: **10** Minutes

Cook Time: **20** Minutes

Total Time: **30** Minutes

INGREDIENTS

- 2 delicata squashes
- 2 tablespoons olive oil
- 1 tsp curry powder
- 1 tsp salt

DIRECTIONS

1. Preheat the oven to 400 F
2. Cut everything in half lengthwise
3. Toss everything with olive oil and place onto a prepared baking sheet
4. Roast for 18-20 minutes at 400 F or until golden brown
5. When ready remove from the oven and serve

Serves: *2*

Prep Time: *10*   Minutes

Cook Time: *20*   Minutes

Total Time: *30*   Minutes

INGREDIENTS

- 1 lb. potatoes
- 1 tsp salt
- 1 tsp paprika
- 1 tablespoon olive oil

DIRECTIONS

1. Preheat the oven to 425 F
2. In a bowl toss everything with olive oil and seasoning
3. Spread everything onto a prepared baking sheet
4. Bake for 8-10 minutes or until crisp
5. When ready remove from the oven and serve

PIZZA

ZUCCHINI PIZZA

Serves: *6-8*

Prep Time: *10*   Minutes

Cook Time: *15*   Minutes

Total Time: *25*   Minutes

INGREDIENTS

- 1 pizza crust
- ½ cup tomato sauce
- ¼ black pepper
- 1 cup zucchini slices
- 1 cup mozzarella cheese
- 1 cup olives

DIRECTIONS

1. Spread tomato sauce on the pizza crust
2. Place all the toppings on the pizza crust
3. Bake the pizza at 425 F for 12-15 minutes
4. When ready remove pizza from the oven and serve

Serves: *6-8*

Prep Time: *10*   Minutes

Cook Time: *15*   Minutes

Total Time: *25*   Minutes

INGREDIENTS

- 1 pizza crust
- 200 g prosciutto
- Basil leaves
- 1 cup tomato sauce
- 1 cup mozzarella
- 1 cup tomato slices

DIRECTIONS

1. Spread tomato sauce on the pizza crust
2. Place all the toppings on the pizza crust
3. Bake the pizza at 425 F for 12-15 minutes
4. When ready remove pizza from the oven and serve

Serves: *6-8*
Prep Time: *10*   Minutes

Cook Time: *15*   Minutes

Total Time: *25*   Minutes

INGREDIENTS

- 1 pizza crust
- 1 cup tomato sauce
- 1 tablespoon olive oil
- 1 cup mozzarella

DIRECTIONS

1. Spread tomato sauce on the pizza crust
2. Place all the toppings on the pizza crust
3. Bake the pizza at 425 F for 12-15 minutes
4. When ready remove pizza from the oven and serve

Serves: *6-8*
Prep Time: *10*   Minutes

Cook Time: *15*   Minutes

Total Time: *25*   Minutes

INGREDIENTS

- 1 pizza crust
- 1 cup marinara sauce
- 1 tsp parprika
- 1 red onion
- 1 cup roasted red peppers
- 1 cup crumbled feta cheese
- 1 cup arugula
- 1 cup mozzarella

DIRECTIONS

1. Spread tomato sauce on the pizza crust
2. Place all the toppings on the pizza crust
3. Bake the pizza at 425 F for 12-15 minutes
4. When ready remove pizza from the oven and serve

FOURTH COOKBOOK

ROASTED SQUASH

Serves:	*3-4*
Prep Time:	*10* Minutes
Cook Time:	*20* Minutes
Total Time:	*30* Minutes

INGREDIENTS

- 2 delicata squashes
- 2 tablespoons olive oil
- 1 tsp curry powder
- 1 tsp salt

DIRECTIONS

5. Preheat the oven to 400 F
6. Cut everything in half lengthwise
7. Toss everything with olive oil and place onto a prepared baking sheet
8. Roast for 18-20 minutes at 400 F or until golden brown
9. When ready remove from the oven and serve

ROASTED CARROT

Serves: **3-4**

Prep Time: **10**   Minutes

Cook Time: **20**   Minutes

Total Time: **30**   Minutes

INGREDIENTS

- 1 lb. carrot
- 2 tablespoons olive oil
- 1 tsp curry powder
- 1 tsp salt

DIRECTIONS

1. **Preheat the oven to 400 F**
2. **Cut everything in half lengthwise**
3. **Toss everything with olive oil and place onto a prepared baking sheet**
4. **Roast for 18-20 minutes at 400 F or until golden brown**
5. **When ready remove from the oven and serve**

SOUP RECIPES

ZUCCHINI SOUP

Serves: *4*

Prep Time: *10*   Minutes

Cook Time: *20*   Minutes

Total Time: *30*   Minutes

INGREDIENTS

- 1 tablespoon olive oil
- 1 lb. zucchini
- ¼ red onion
- ½ cup all-purpose flour
- ¼ tsp salt
- ¼ tsp pepper
- 1 can vegetable broth
- 1 cup heavy cream

DIRECTIONS

1. In a saucepan heat olive oil and sauté zucchini until tender
2. Add remaining ingredients to the saucepan and bring to a boil
3. When all the vegetables are tender transfer to a blender and blend until smooth
4. Pour soup into bowls, garnish with parsley and serve

SIDE DISHES

CHICKEN NUGGETS

Serves: *3*

Prep Time: *10*   Minutes

Cook Time: *25*   Minutes

Total Time: *35*   Minutes

INGREDIENTS

- 2 chicken breasts
- ¼ cup almond flour
- 1 tablespoon seasoning
- 1 tablespoon olive oil
- ½ tsp salt
- ¼ tsp pepper

DIRECTIONS

1. Preheat the oven to 375 F
2. In a bowl add seasoning, salt, almond flour, pepper
3. Add pieces of chicken breast into your bowl and cover with flour
4. Transfer to your baking sheet
5. Bake 18-20 minutes, remove and serve

BEEF FAJITAS

Serves: *3*

Prep Time: *10*   Minutes

Cook Time: *20*   Minutes

Total Time: *30*   Minutes

INGREDIENTS

- 1 lb. beef stir-fry strips
- 1 red onion
- 1 red bell pepper
- ¼ tsp tsp cumin
- ¼ tsp chili powder
- salt
- pepper
- 1 avocado

DIRECTIONS

1. In a skillet add strips and stir-fry, add salt, pepper and cook for 2-3 minute and set aside
2. Add onions, bell peppers, chili powder, cumin and fry for 2-3 minutes
3. Remove to a plate and serve with avocado

SUMMER SALMON

Serves: *4*
Prep Time: *10*   Minutes

Cook Time: *30*   Minutes

Total Time: *40*   Minutes

INGREDIENTS

- 3 salmon fillets
- 2 leeks
- 6 oz. asparagus spears
- 1 cup sugar snap peas
- 3 tablespoons white wine
- 1 cup vegetable broth
- 1 tablespoon chives
- salt

DIRECTIONS

1. In a Dutch oven add salmon, asparagus, wine, peas, chicken bean and pepper
2. Bring to boil and simmer for 12-15 minutes
3. Sprinkle with chives and serve

GRILLED SALMON

Serves: *4*

Prep Time: *10*   Minutes

Cook Time: *20*   Minutes

Total Time: *30*   Minutes

INGREDIENTS

- Juice of 1 lime
- 2 tablespoons basil
- 3 salmon fillets
- 2 tablespoons salmon fillets
- 2 cup low-fat yogurt
- 1 tablespoon mayonnaise
- ½ tsp lime zest
- salt
- mixed salad leaves

DIRECTIONS

1. In a bowl mix pepper, basil, lime juice, salt and pepper
2. Add salmon fillets and let it marinade for 20-30 minutes
3. In another bowl mix lime zest, basil, mayonnaise, yogurt and salt
4. Preheat the oven to 400 F and place the salmon fillets on a ridged grill pan
5. Brush the salmon with marinade and grill for 4-5 minutes per side
6. When ready remove and serve

Serves: *12*

Prep Time: *10* Minutes

Cook Time: *20* Minutes

Total Time: *30* Minutes

INGREDIENTS

- 1 lemon
- juice 1 lime
- 1 tablespoon olive oil
- 1 tsp honey
- 1 garlic clove
- 1 tablespoon oregano
- 1 tablespoon parsley
- 6 oz. monkfish fillet
- 12 fresh mussels
- 1 yellow bell pepper
- 1 zucchini
- 12 cherry tomatoes
- salt

DIRECTIONS

1. In a bowl add lime juice, honey, lemon zest, garlic, oregano and salt and mix well, marinade for 50-60 minutes
2. Prepare 10-12 wooden skewers and add on each one skewer 1 cube of monkfish, 1 piece of bell pepper, 1 zucchini, 1 mussel and a cherry tomato
3. Grill each kebab for 10-12 minutes or until done
4. When ready, remove and serve

<h1 style="text-align:center">POTATO TORTILLA</h1>

Serves: **6**

Prep Time: **10**   Minutes

Cook Time: **20**   Minutes

Total Time: **30**   Minutes

INGREDIENTS

- **1,5 lb. potatoes**

- 1 tablespoon olive oil
- 1 red onion
- 1 zucchini
- 1 slice turkey bacon
- 5 eggs
- 1 tablespoon parsley
- pepper

DIRECTIONS

1. In a saucepan add potato cubes, water and bring to a boil
2. In a skillet add potatoes, bacon, zucchini and cook until potatoes are tender
3. In a bowl beat the eggs, add water, pepper, parsley, pour the egg mixture over the vegetables and cook for 4-5 minutes
4. Slide the tortilla onto a plate, cool for 2-3 minutes and cut into wedges and serve

ASIAN STIR-FRY

Serves: 2
Prep Time: 10 Minutes

Cook Time: 10 Minutes

Total Time: 20 Minutes

INGREDIENTS

- ½ lb. dried noodles

- 1 lb. Asian stir-fry vegetables

- ½ cups hoisin sauce

- 1 tsp chili flakes

DIRECTIONS

1. In a frying pan add vegetables, water and stir-fry for 4-5 minutes
2. Add hoisin sauce, noodles, chili flakes and toss to coat, remove and serve

APRICOT CHICKEN PATTIES

Serves: **4**
Prep Time: **10**   Minutes

Cook Time: **10**   Minutes

Total Time: **20**   Minutes

INGREDIENTS

- 1 lb. chicken mince

- 2 slices bread

- 3 oz. pistachio nuts

- 1/3 lb. dried apricots

DIRECTIONS

1. In a bowl mix combine the mince, apricots, bread, pistachios and season with pepper
2. Roll into o4 patties and cook for 4-5 minutes per side
3. Remove and serve

GREEN PESTO PASTA

Serves:	2	
Prep Time:	5	Minutes
Cook Time:	15	Minutes
Total Time:	20	Minutes

INGREDIENTS

- 4 oz. spaghetti
- 2 cups basil leaves
- 2 garlic cloves
- ¼ cup olive oil
- 2 tablespoons parmesan cheese

- ½ tsp black pepper

DIRECTIONS

1. Bring water to a boil and add pasta
2. In a blend add parmesan cheese, basil leaves, garlic and blend
3. Add olive oil, pepper and blend again
4. Pour pesto onto pasta and serve when ready

SALMON WITH ROSEMAY

Serves: 2

Prep Time: *10*   Minutes

Cook Time: *10*   Minutes

Total Time: *20*   Minutes

INGREDIENTS

- 3 Atlantic salmon fillets
- 2 tsp olive oil
- 1 clove garlic
- 1 tablespoon rosemary
- black pepper
- 1 tablespoon lemon juice
- 1 tablespoon white wine

DIRECTIONS

1. In a frying pan sauté garlic, rosemary and pepper for 1-2 minutes
2. Add fish and cook for 1-2 minutes per side

MUSHROOM BURGERS

Serves: 2

Prep Time: *10*   Minutes

Cook Time: *10*   Minutes

Total Time: *20*   Minutes

INGREDIENTS

-    2 tablespoons olive oil
-    1 lb. mushrooms
-    1 lb. beef mince
-    1 onion
-    1 tsp Worcestershire sauce
-    1 egg
-    4 hamburger buns
-    1 cup lettuce
-    4 slices tomatoes

-   salt

DIRECTIONS

1. In a frying pan add mushrooms and cook for 4-5 minutes, remove and set aside
2. In a bowl mix beef mince, salt, pepper, Worcestershire sauce, mushrooms, onion and mix well
3. Form into 2 patties, and refrigerate for 10-15 minutes
4. In a frying pan cook patty for 2-3 minutes per side and also grill hamburger buns
5. Top buns with lettuce, tomatoes and patties
6. Serve when ready

BLACK BEANS BURGERS

Serves: *4*

Prep Time: *10*   Minutes

Cook Time: *20*   Minutes

Total Time: *30*   Minutes

INGREDIENTS

- 1 lb. black beans
- 1 cup brown rice
- 1 onion
- 1 onion
- ¼ tsp tabasco sauce
- 1 egg
- ½ cup bread crumbs
- 5 tablespoons salsa
- 4 hamburger buns
- ½ cups yoghurt
- 4 leaves romaine lettuce

- 1 avocado

DIRECTIONS

1. Preheat the oven to 325 F
2. In a bowl mix mashed beans, onions, tabasco sauce, rice, egg, breadcrumbs and mix well
3. Divide mixture into patties and bake for 12-15 minutes or until done
4. In another bowl mix yoghurt and salsa, serve with lettuce and avocado

CABBAGE FRITATTA

Serves: **2**

Prep Time: **10**   Minutes

Cook Time: **20**   Minutes

Total Time: **30**   Minutes

INGREDIENTS

- ½ lb. cabbage
- 1 tablespoon olive oil
- ½ red onion
- 2 eggs
- ¼ tsp salt
- 2 oz. cheddar cheese
- 1 garlic clove
- ¼ tsp dill

DIRECTIONS

1. In a bowl whisk eggs with salt and cheese

2. In a frying pan heat olive oil and pour egg mixture

3. Add remaining ingredients and mix well

4. Serve when ready

BRUSSEL SPROUTS FRITATTA

Serves: **2**

Prep Time: **10**   Minutes

Cook Time: **20**   Minutes

Total Time: **30**   Minutes

INGREDIENTS

- ½ lb. Brussel sprouts
- 1 tablespoon olive oil
- ½ red onion
- ¼ tsp salt
- 2 eggs
- 2 oz. cheddar cheese
- 1 garlic clove
- ¼ tsp dill

DIRECTIONS

1. In a skillet sauté Brussel sprouts until tender

2. In a bowl whisk eggs with salt and cheese

3. In a frying pan heat olive oil and pour egg mixture

4. Add remaining ingredients and mix well

5. Serve when ready

CELERY FRITATTA

Serves: *2*
Prep Time: *10* Minutes

Cook Time: *20* Minutes

Total Time: *30* Minutes

INGREDIENTS

- 1 cup celery
- 1 tablespoon olive oil
- ½ red onion
- ¼ tsp salt
- 2 eggs
- 2 oz. cheddar cheese
- 1 garlic clove
- ¼ tsp dill

DIRECTIONS

1. In a bowl whisk eggs with salt and cheese
2. In a frying pan heat olive oil and pour egg mixture
3. Add remaining ingredients and mix well
4. When ready serve with sautéed celery

Serves: 2

Prep Time: *10*   Minutes

Cook Time: *20*   Minutes

Total Time: *30*   Minutes

INGREDIENTS

- 8-10 slices prosciutto
- 1 tsp rosemary
- 1 tablespoon olive oil
- ½ red onion
- ¼ tsp salt
- 2 eggs
- 2 oz. parmesan cheese
- 1 garlic clove
- ¼ tsp dill

DIRECTIONS

1. In a bowl whisk eggs with salt and parmesan cheese
2. In a frying pan heat olive oil and pour egg mixture
3. Add remaining ingredients and mix well

4. When prosciutto and eggs are cooked remove from heat and
    serve

OREGANO FRITATTA

Serves: 2
Prep Time: 10   Minutes

Cook Time: 20   Minutes

Total Time: 30   Minutes

INGREDIENTS

-   1 tsp oregano
-   1 tablespoon olive oil
-   ½ red onion
-   ¼ tsp salt
-   2 eggs
-   2 oz. cheddar cheese
-   1 garlic clove
-   ¼ tsp dill

DIRECTIONS

1. In a bowl whisk eggs with salt and cheese
2. In a frying pan heat olive oil and pour egg mixture
3. Add remaining ingredients and mix well
4. Serve when ready

Serves: 2
Prep Time: 5   Minutes
Cook Time: 5   Minutes
Total Time: *10*   Minutes

INGREDIENTS

- 1 cup cooked brown rice
- 1 gluten-free tortilla
- 2-3 tablespoons hummus
- ¼ cup black beans
- ¼ cup tomatoes
- ¼ cup cucumber
- ¼ cup avocado
- ¼ cup romaine lettuce

DIRECTIONS

1. Microwave the tortilla for 20-30 seconds
2. Spread hummus on tortilla
3. Add beans, tomatoes, cucumber, and remaining ingredients
4. Roll like a burrito and serve

Serves: **4-6**

Prep Time: **10**   Minutes

Cook Time: **30**   Minutes

Total Time: **40**   Minutes

INGREDIENTS

- 2 white potatoes
- 1 tsp olive oil
- 1 tsp garlic powder
- 1 tsp onion powder
- salt
- 1 cup avocado dip

DIRECTIONS

1. Slice potatoes into thick slices
2. In a bowl combine garlic powder, onion powder, salt, olive oil and mix well
3. Place the potatoes into the mixture and stir to coat
4. Bake the potatoes at 425 F for 25-30 minutes
5. When ready remove from the oven and serve with avocado dip

Serves: *4*

Prep Time: *10*   Minutes

Cook Time: *15*   Minutes

Total Time: *25*   Minutes

INGREDIENTS

- 2 cups kale
- 1 tablespoon avocado oil
- 1 tsp salt
- 1 tsp turmeric
- 1 tsp chili powder
- 1 tsp curry powder

DIRECTIONS

1. In a bowl combine all ingredients except kale
2. Mix well and add kale to the seasoning mixture
3. Toss to coat and then place the kale in a baking dish
4. Bake at 250 F for 12-15 minutes
5. When ready remove from the oven and serve

Serves: *2*
Prep Time: *10*   Minutes

Cook Time: *20*   Minutes

Total Time: *30*   Minutes

INGREDIENTS

- 1 tablespoon olive oil
- 1 clove garlic
- 1 lb. pork
- ½ red onion
- 1 cup carrot
- 1 cabbage
- ½ cup soy sauce
- ¼ tsp black pepper

DIRECTIONS

1. In a skillet sauté garlic and onion until soft
2. Add pork, cabbage and cook for another 6-7 minutes
3. Add soy sauce, carrot and cook until vegetables are tender
4. When ready transfer mixture to a bowl, add pepper and serve

Serves: **1**

Prep Time: **10** Minutes

Cook Time: **20** Minutes

Total Time: **30** Minutes

INGREDIENTS

- 1 tablespoon olive oil
- 1 chicken breast
- 1 tsp oregano
- 1 tsp black pepper
- 1 cup tomatoes
- ¼ cucumber
- ¼ cup red onion
- ¼ cup black olives
- 1/4 cup feta cheese
- 1 cup dressing

DIRECTIONS

1. In a skillet add chicken and cook until golden
2. Add seasoning and onion
3. When ready place all ingredients in a bowl
4. Drizzle dressing on top, mix well and serve

Serves: 2
Prep Time: 5   Minutes

Cook Time: 15   Minutes

Total Time: 20   Minutes

INGREDIENTS

- ½ cup celery
- 1 packet Knox Gelatin
- 1 cup cranberry juice
- 1 can berry cranberry sauce
- 1 cup sour cream

DIRECTIONS

1. In a pan add juice, gelatin, cranberry sauce and cook on low heat
2. Add sour cream, celery and continue to cook
3. Pour mixture into a pan
4. Serve when ready

Serves: *4*

Prep Time: *10*   Minutes

Cook Time: *30*   Minutes

Total Time: *40*   Minutes

INGREDIENTS

- ½ lb. cherry tomatoes
- ½ cucumber
- 3 oz. cooked quinoa
- 1 tsp bouillon powder
- 2 spring onions
- 1 red pepper
- ½ avocado
- 1 pack Japanese tofu

DIRECTIONS

1. **In a bowl combine all ingredients together**
2. **Add salad dressing, toss well and serve**

Serves: *4*

Prep Time: *10*   Minutes

Cook Time: *30*   Minutes

Total Time: *40*   Minutes

INGREDIENTS

- 1 tsp olive oil
- ¼ lb. tomatoes
- 2 oz. radish
- 1 oz. parsley
- 1 tablespoon coriander
- salt

DIRECTIONS

1. In a bowl combine all ingredients together and mix well
2. Add salad dressing, toss well and serve

Serves: *1*

Prep Time: *5*   Minutes

Cook Time: *5*   Minutes

Total Time: *10*   Minutes

INGREDIENTS

- ¼ cup zucchini
- ¼ cup red capsicum
- ½ cup yellow capsicum
- 1 cup sprouted moong
- ¼ cup apple
- 1 tablespoon olive oil
- 1 tsp lemon juice

DIRECTIONS

1. In a bowl combine all ingredients together and mix well
2. Add olive oil, toss well and serve

Serves: *1*

Prep Time: *5*   Minutes

Cook Time: *5*   Minutes

Total Time: *10*   Minutes

INGREDIENTS

- ¼ cooked quinoa
- ¼ cup avocado
- ¼ cup zucchini
- ¼ cup capsicum cubes
- ¼ cup mushroom
- ½ cup cherry tomatoes
- 1 cup lettuce
- 1 tablespoon sprouts
- 1 tsp olive oil
- Salad dressing

DIRECTIONS

1. In a bowl combine all ingredients together and mix well
2. Add salad dressing, toss well and serve

Serves: *1*

Prep Time: *5*   Minutes

Cook Time: *5*   Minutes

Total Time: *10* Minutes

INGREDIENTS

- 1 pack tofu
- 1 cup chopped vegetables (carrots, cucumber)

DRESSING

- 1 tablespoon sesame oil
- 1 tablespoon mustard
- 1 tablespoon brown rice vinegar
- 1 tablespoon soya sauce

DIRECTIONS

1. In a bowl combine all ingredients together and mix well
2. Add salad dressing, toss well and serve

Serves: *1*

Prep Time: 5   Minutes

Cook Time: 5   Minutes

Total Time: *10*   Minutes

INGREDIENTS

- ¼ lb. rice noodles
- 1 red pepper
- 1 onion
- 4 stalks coriander
- ¼ package silken tofu
- 1 oz. roasted peanuts
- Salad dressing

DIRECTIONS

1. In a bowl combine all ingredients together and mix well
2. Add salad dressing, toss well and serve

Serves: *1*

Prep Time: *5*   Minutes

Cook Time: *5*   Minutes

Total Time: *10*   Minutes

INGREDIENTS

- 2 avocados
- ¼ lb. snap peas
- 1 tablespoon sesame seeds

SALAD DRESSING

- 1 tablespoon soya sauce
- 1 tablespoon umeboshi puree
- 2 tablespoons mikawa mirin

DIRECTIONS

1. **In a bowl combine all ingredients together and mix well**
2. **Add salad dressing, toss well and serve**

Serves: *1*
Prep Time: **5**   Minutes

Cook Time: **5**   Minutes

Total Time: **10** Minutes

INGREDIENTS

- ½ lb. mushrooms
- 1 clove garlic
- ½ lb. salad leaves
- ¼ lb. tofu
- 1 oz. walnuts
- salad dressing

DIRECTIONS

1. In a bowl combine all ingredients together and mix well
2. Add salad dressing, toss well and serve

Serves: *1*

Prep Time: *5*   Minutes

Cook Time: *5*   Minutes

Total Time: *10*   Minutes

INGREDIENTS

- 2 cucumbers
- 3 radishes
- ¼ red bell pepper
- 2 spring onions
- 1 tablespoon red wine vinegar
- 1 tablespoon rice vinegar
- 1 tablespoon soya sauce
- 1 tablespoon clearspring mirin
- 2 cups mixed salad greens

DIRECTIONS

1. In a bowl combine all ingredients together and mix well
2. Add salad dressing, toss well and serve

QUINOA SALAD

Serves: *1*

Prep Time: *5*   Minutes

Cook Time: *5*   Minutes

Total Time: *10*   Minutes

INGREDIENTS

- 1 cup cooked quinoa
- ¼ cup clearspring hijiki
- ¼ red bell pepper
- 1 bun watercress
- 2 radishes
- 2 tablespoons goji berries

DIRECTIONS

1. In a bowl combine all ingredients together and mix well
2. Add salad dressing, toss well and serve

FISH STEW

Serves: **4**

Prep Time: **15**   Minutes

Cook Time: **45**   Minutes

Total Time: **60**   Minutes

INGREDIENTS

- 1 fennel bulb
- 1 red onion
- 2 garlic cloves
- 2 tablespoons olive oil
- 1 cup white wine
- 1 tablespoon fennel seeds
- 4 bay leaves
- 2 cups chicken stock
- 8 oz. halibut
- 12 oz. haddock

DIRECTIONS

1. Chop all ingredients in big chunks
2. In a large pot heat olive oil and add ingredients one by one
3. Cook for 5-6 or until slightly brown

4. Add remaining ingredients and cook until tender, 35-45 minutes

5. Season while stirring on low heat

6. When ready remove from heat and serve

Serves: *4*

Prep Time: *15*   Minutes

Cook Time: *45*   Minutes

Total Time: *60*   Minutes

INGREDIENTS

- 2 tablespoons olive oil
- 2 red onions
- 2 cloves garlic
- 1. Tablespoon rosemary
- 1 tablespoon thyme
- 2 lb. beef
- 1 cup white wine
- 1 cup butternut squash
- 2 cups beef broth
- ½ cup tomatoes
-

DIRECTIONS

1. Chop all ingredients in big chunks
2. In a large pot heat olive oil and add ingredients one by one
3. Cook for 5-6 or until slightly brown
4. Add remaining ingredients and cook until tender, 35-45 minutes

5. Season while stirring on low heat

6. When ready remove from heat and serve

BACON CASSEROLE

Serves: *4*

Prep Time: *10*   Minutes

Cook Time: *15*   Minutes

Total Time: *25*   Minutes

INGREDIENTS

- 4-5 slices bacon
- 3-4 tablespoons butter
- 5-6 tablespoons flour
- 2 cups milk
- 3 cups cheddar cheese
- 2 cups chicken breast
- 1 tsp seasoning mix

DIRECTIONS

1. Sauté the veggies and set aside
2. Preheat the oven to 425 F
3. Transfer the sautéed veggies to a baking dish, add remaining ingredients to the baking dish
4. Mix well, add seasoning and place the dish in the oven
5. Bake for 12-15 minutes or until slightly brown

6.   When ready remove from the oven and serve

Serves: *4*
Prep Time: *10*   Minutes

Cook Time: **25**   Minutes

Total Time: **35**   Minutes

INGREDIENTS

- 1 tablespoon olive oil
- 1 red onion
- 1 bell pepper
- 2 cloves garlic
- 1 can black beans
- 1 cup chicken
- 1 can green chilis
- 1 can enchilada sauce
- 1 cup cheddar cheese
- 1 cup sour cream

DIRECTIONS

1. Sauté the veggies and set aside
2. Preheat the oven to 425 F
3. Transfer the sautéed veggies to a baking dish, add remaining ingredients to the baking dish
4. Mix well, add seasoning and place the dish in the oven

5. Bake for 15-25 minutes or until slightly brown

6. When ready remove from the oven and serve

CASSEROLE PIZZA

Serves: *6-8*

Prep Time: *10*   Minutes

Cook Time: *15*   Minutes

Total Time: *25*   Minutes

INGREDIENTS

- 1 pizza crust
- ½ cup tomato sauce
- ¼ black pepper
- 1 cup zucchini slices
- 1 cup mozzarella cheese
- 1 cup olives

DIRECTIONS

1. Spread tomato sauce on the pizza crust
2. Place all the toppings on the pizza crust
3. Bake the pizza at 425 F for 12-15 minutes
4. When ready remove pizza from the oven and serve

THANK YOU FOR READING THIS BOOK!

CPSIA information can be obtained
at www.ICGtesting.com
Printed in the USA
BVHW070121090421
604476BV00001B/134

9 781664 033702